THE EAST KENT R.
and the Knees Woodland Minia
by Jonathan James

INTRODUCTION

People often associate Kent with hops and apple trees, and maybe as the gateway to Europe. It is easy to forget that the county once had heavy industry including a thriving coal field. Whilst the coal mines have all now closed, the East Kent Railway remains as a reminder of the county's industrial past.

Tucked away in a corner of Kent, not far from Dover, and nearer to France than London, is the East Kent Railway.

The railway operates a two-mile section of what was once a much larger system, which was originally constructed to serve the Kent coalfields, but also provided a limited passenger and freight service for local communities along the line.

The railway closed in the mid-1980s following the demise of the Kent coal industry, but preservationists soon stepped in to rescue a short section of the railway and some of the rolling stock from the nearby collieries.

Passenger services resumed in 1995 between Shepherdswell and Eythorne using a heritage diesel unit.

2020 was due to be a celebration of 25-years of passenger operations, but events have been overtaken by the Coronavirus, which forced the railway to close for most of the season. As with most preserved railways, the main income is from passenger fares, which has placed the East Kent Railway in a challenging position.

The purpose of this book is to celebrate 25-years of passenger services and raise funds for the railway to help it through the current crisis. The railway is expected to reopen on 1 August 2020 and I encourage you to pay a visit.

There are a number of people who have helped me with preparing this book including Peter Scott, Danni Macey, Peter Wilson and Phil Barnes as well as Dave Harris and Matthew Plews from the East Kent Railway. Any errors which remain are my responsibility, for which I apologise in advance.

Jonathan James, July 2020

The Class 108 unit used for the opening train, seen at Shepherdswell in the early days of the railway in Network South East livery, The Class 107 unit, in Strathclyde livery, is standing behind. The Class 107 unit was based at the railway between 1992 and 1996.
Dave Harris / EKR

THE EAST KENT RAILWAY

The East Kent Railway was constructed between 1911 and 1917 to serve the Kent coalfields. The railway was originally envisaged as a 'Y' shaped network linking Shepherdswell, Canterbury and Richborough, with a junction at Eastry, and branches to serve various collieries. The section between Canterbury Road and Canterbury was never completed, nor were most of the colliery branches (as the collieries they were planned to serve were never sunk). An unusual feature of the railway is Golgotha tunnel, which was constructed for double-track, but to reduce costs the trackbed of the second line was never fully excavated.

The famous light railway promoter and engineer, Colonel H.F. Stephens, was Manager of the railway until his death in 1931, when his assistant W.H. Austen took over and ran the railway until nationalisation in 1948.

Passenger services were always sparse and operated between 1916 and 1948. Station facilities were very basic, usually consisting of a short platform and basic waiting shelter. Not surprisingly, passenger numbers were very low, with only 556 passenger journeys originating from the East Kent Railway in 1947.

The majority of the coal mines, that the railway was built to serve, were not a commercial success, with only Tilmanstone Colliery generating any significant traffic, although other goods traffic was carried on the railway. The railway saw some military use in World War II, when rail-mounted guns were based at stations along the line.

The line between Eastry and Richborough officially closed in 1949, although the line had not been in regular use for several years. The line between Eastry and Canterbury Road was closed in 1950, shortly followed by the Tilmanstone Colliery to Eastry section in 1951. The remaining railway continued to carry coal traffic between Tilmanstone Colliery and the main line at Shepherdswell until closure of the mine in 1986, with the line officially closing in 1987.

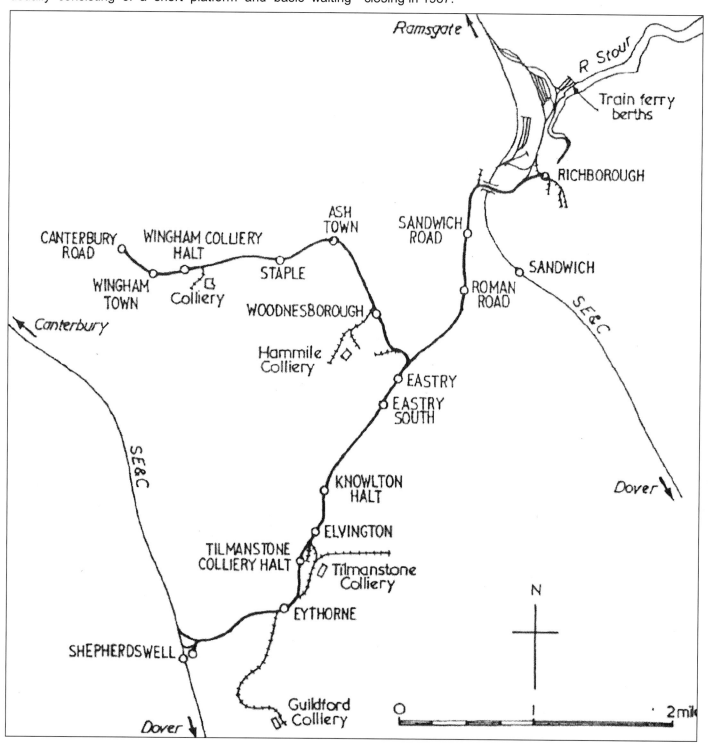

25 YEARS OF HERITAGE OPERATION

The East Kent Railway Society was formed in November 1985 to preserve the remaining section of the East Kent Railway. Work started on clearing the trackbed in 1989 and in 1993 a Light Railway Order was obtained, which enabled the first passenger service to operate between Shepherdswell and Eythorne on 24 June 1995. In 2003, the East Kent Railway became a Charitable Trust.

New platforms were constructed at both Shepherdswell and Eythorne stations before passenger services could commence. Steam trains returned to the railway on 24 August 1996, during a 'Return of Steam' weekend.

The railway facilities have gradually been improved over the years, including a small museum at Shepherdswell station, a model railway and café facilities. Trains occasionally operate beyond Eythorne station to Wigmore Lane. There are long-term plans to extend the railway from a junction at Eythorne towards the unsuccessful Guilford Colliery.

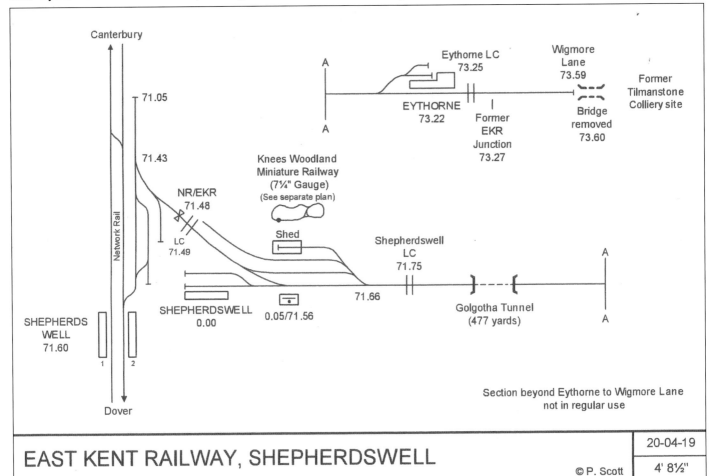

EAST KENT RAILWAY, SHEPHERDSWELL

20-04-19

© P. Scott

4' 8½"

Copyright Peter Scott

Class 09 D4113 shunts around the curve that once linked the EKR with British Railways at Shepherdswell on 7 September 2014.

Phil Barnes

Above: The East Kent Railway station is a few minutes' walk from Shepherdswell main line station, which is served by Southeastern trains between Dover Priory and London Victoria. The main line station building is seen on 30th August 2015.

Below: 375305 arriving at Shepherdswell from London Victoria on 30 August 2015. The original connection to the East Kent Railway was behind the train on the right-hand side of the view.

Both: Author

Above: There is a display of former mining wagons and other railway equipment along the approach road, which leads to the 3½ / 5-inch gauge elevated miniature railway, toilets, café and picnic area. Here we see the 'Colonels Café' and play area looking towards the site entrance and 5-inch gauge miniature railway, on 17 April 2016.

Below: A short walk beyond the café takes visitors to a viewing area, the trolleybus, the model railway coach, the Knees Woodlands and the Knees Woodland Miniature Railway. The route involves crossing the connection with Network Rail infrastructure, which was once used by coal trains from Tilmanstone colliery. Country walks are available through the Knees Woodland, which is owned by the railway. A separate path takes you down to the Visitors Centre and the station platform, which was reconstructed by railway volunteers prior to passenger services commencing in 1995. The Shepherdswell Station sign is seen on 19 May 2019.

Both: Author

Above: A view of Shepherdswell station platform, with the 5-inch gauge miniature railway station seen on the hill behind, and AD427 THE BUFFS in the siding, taken on 17 April 2016.

Below: The approach to Shepherdswell, with NS687 and SNOWDOWN in view, also on 17 April 2016.

Both: Author

Above: After departure from Shepherdswell trains pass Shepherdswell Signal Box and stabling sidings, where rolling stock can be seen under restoration. A view towards Eythorne from the end of the platform at Shepherdswell on 17 April 2016.

Left: Shepherdswell signal box seen on 19 May 2019.

Both: Author

Not long after leaving Shepherdswell, trains pass over North Bank level crossing before reaching Golgotha Tunnel. The tunnel is 477 yards long and was constructed to accommodate two tracks, although only part of the tunnel was fully excavated. Trains then make their way through the Kent countryside, before passing the site of a junction with a branch line to Guilford Colliery (also referred to as Guildford Colliery), shortly before arriving at Eythorne which is just under two miles from Shepherdswell.

Author

Above: 09025 and 2-EPB 5759 arriving at Eythorne on 15 June 2014.

Below: Class 101/108 DMU shortly after arriving at Eythorne on 17 April 2016.

Both: Author

Above: Eythorne has a through platform and a bay platform that is generally used for stabling rolling stock, with a café located in one of the wagons. There is a small museum in Eythorne signal box, which is open on running days. The railway then passes Shooters Hill level crossing before continuing towards Wigmore Lane. Trains only operate on the section between Eythorne and Wigmore Lane on special events. This view of Eythorne station was taken from a train on 15 June 2014. The line to Wigmore Lane continues beyond the level crossing gates seen in the distance.

Below: A view from Eythorne with the line towards Wigmore Lane bearing right on 17 April 2016. The line towards Eastry used to carry straight on from this point.

Both: Author

Above: 09025 in Connex livery is seen crossing Shooters Hill at Eythorne on 19 May 2013.

Left: The end of the line at Wigmore Lane on 14 March 2013.

Both: Peter Wilson Collection

VISITOR CENTRE, MUSEUM & MODEL RAILWAY

Above: There is a Visitor Centre at Shepherdswell opposite the station entrance, which utilises a signal box from Barham station from the nearby Elham Valley Line. The signal box was built in 1887 and was acquired from Barham in 1931 when the line from Lyminge to Canterbury was singled. Arter Bros motor and agricultural engineers bought it in 1931, and first used it as a motor cycle showroom and later as a parts store. It was moved to Shepherdswell in 2002, when it was converted into the Visitor Centre. The Elham Valley Line itself closed in 1947. It is seen on 19 May 2019.

Below: The interior of the Visitor Centre, which includes a map of the railway. The lever frame is from Folkestone West ground frame.
Both: Author

Above: The Walmer Model Railway Group have constructed several model railways in a former LMS Stanier coach, which is stabled at Shepherdswell station and is open on running days. It is pictured on 19 May 2019.

Below: A selection of artifacts were displayed in a wagon at Eythorne station, but this has since been removed. The photo is dated 17 April 2016.

Both: Author

In 1996 the signal box from Selling station near Faversham was moved to Eythorne station, where it was converted into a museum, which is usually open on running days These two views show it (*above, Phil Barnes*) on 3 June 2002, and (*below, Author*) on 18 November 2012.

ROLLING STOCK

CURRENT STEAM LOCOMOTIVES

Name	Works Number	Builder	Type	Built	Comments
ST DUNSTAN	2004	Avonside	0-6-0ST	1927	Ex-Snowdown Colliery, Kent
ACHILLES	2087	Peckett	0-4-0ST	1948	On long-term loan to the railway
ST = Saddle Tank					

ST DUNSTAN was built by the Avonside Locomotive Company in 1927 and worked at Snowdown Colliery in Kent until it was withdrawn. The locomotive was then moved to a private preservation site at Sellindge in Kent, before moving to the East Kent Railway in 1992. ST DUNSTAN is being repaired and repainted, pending funding for a full restoration. It is seen here at Snowdown Colliery in the mid-1970s.

Andrew Kirkham

ST DUNSTAN seen at Eythorne in 2004 after repainting in blue livery.
Peter Wilson Collection

Now painted black, ST DUNSTAN is seen at Shepherdswell on 15 June 2014.
Author

On 25 March 2018 ST DUNSTAN is seen at Shepherdswell.
Peter Wilson Collection

Above: ACHILLES was built by Peckett and Sons in 1948 and has had a rather nomadic life, having worked in Flint, Wolverhampton and Preston, and was originally named DAFYDD. After being withdrawn from service ACHILLES was based at the Lytham Creek Motive Power Depot, before moving to the Lakeside and Haverthwaite Railway and then to the Buckinghamshire Railway Society at Quainton Road. In January 2018 she moved to the Mangapps Farm Railway Museum in Essex. In 2019 she visited the East Kent Railway and operated a number of steam-hauled services during the season. ACHILLES returned to the East Kent Railway in 2020 on long-term loan. In this view, the loco is stabled at Shepherdswell on 19 May 2019.

Author

Below: ACHILLES approaching Farm Crossing on 6 May 2019.

Peter Wilson Collection

CURRENT DIESEL LOCOMOTIVES

Name	Number	Builder	Type	Built	Comments
SNOWDOWN	416002	Fowler	0-4-0DM	1952	Ex-Snowdown Colliery, Kent
	01530	Thomas Hill	0-4-0DH	1977	Ex-Ministry of Defence, Kineton
	01546	Thomas Hill	0-4-0DH	1977	Ex-Ministry of Defence, Kineton
RICHBOROUGH CASTLE	D1197	English Electric	0-6-0DH	1967	Ex-Rawdon Colliery, Nottinghamshire
THE BUFFS / 9TH FIELD SQUADRON ROYAL ENGINEERS	AD427	Ruston & Hornsby LSSH Type	0-6-0DH	1961	Ex-Ministry of Defence, Donnington
	08502	British Railways	0-6-0DE	1958	
	08676	British Railways	0-6-0DE	1959	
	08685	British Railways	0-6-0DE	1959	
	08799	British Railways	0-6-0DE	1960	
	08804	British Railways	0-6-0DE	1960	Used for spares
	08742	British Railways	0-6-0DE	1960	Used for spares

DE = Diesel Electric   DM = Diesel Mechanical   DH = Diesel Hydraulic

SNOWDOWN was built by John Fowler of Leeds in 1952 and worked at the nearby Snowdown Colliery, where it is seen on 25 September 1970, before arriving at the East Kent Railway in 1990.

Gordon Edgar

Above: The East Kent Railway is home to two Military of Defence locomotives built by Thomas Hill of Rotherham and which worked for the Ministry of Defence Railway at Kineton. Locomotive number 01530 was built in 1984 and 01546 in 1977. Sister locomotive 01543 was based here for a short time but has now returned to industrial service. 01530 is stabled in the platform at Shepherdswell on 26 January 2020.

Peter Wilson Collection

Below: 01546 is seen at Shepherdswell on 19 May 2019.

Author

Above: RICHBOROUGH CASTLE was built by the English Electric Company in 1967 and worked at Rawdon Colliery in Nottinghamshire until 1984, arriving at the East Kent Railway in November 1990. Here it is seen at Shepherdswell in the early days of the railway.

Peter Wilson Collection

Below: RICHBOROUGH CASTLE is now on static display as the engine is beyond economic repair. This photo shows it at Shepherdswell on 19 May 2019.

Author

Two views of AD427 THE BUFFS / 9TH FIELD SQUADRON ROYAL ENGINEERS at Shepherdswell on 14 July 2019. AD427 was built by Ruston & Hornsby in 1961 (Army Number 8221) and was used by the Ministry of Defence at Donnington. The locomotive is named THE BUFFS in honour of the Royal East Kent Regiment, which was based at Canterbury ('The Buffs' is a reference to their khaki coloured uniform). The guest of honour at the naming ceremony in November 1998 was Major Geoff Giddings, who had been in the 9th Field Squadron of the Royal Engineers, hence the second name.

Both: Phil Barnes

Above: Several Class 08 shunting locomotives are based at the East Kent Railway, a number of which were purchased from English, Welsh and Scottish Railway (EWS). 08502 was built in Doncaster in 1958, 08865 and 08676 were built in Horwich in 1959 and 08799 was built in Derby in 1960. 08804 and 08742 were brought to the East Kent Railway to provide spare parts for the other Class 08s. Still carrying faded EWS livery. 08676 is hauling the VEP coach approaching North Bank level crossing on 6 May 2019.

Peter Wilson Collection

Right: A repainted 08502 sits in the sunshine at Shepherdswell on 14 July 2019.

Phil Barnes

CURRENT DIESEL / DIESEL ELECTRIC MULTIPLE UNITS

Name	Number	Builder	Type	Built	Comments
	142036	BREL	Pacer	1985	Ex- Northern Rail
	142017	BREL	Pacer	1985	Ex- Northern Rail
	60100 (60154) / 60800	British Railways	Class 205	1957	Unit number 1101 / 205001

Class 142 Pacers (not pictured)

A total of 96 Class 142 Pacer units were built by (British Rail Engineering Limited (BREL) between 1985 and 1987 for use on rural lines around the country. The Northern Rail fleet was withdrawn in 2020. The East Kent Railway has purchased units 142017 and 142036, one of which has been delivered to the railway.

The Class 205 Diesel Electric Multiple Unit (DEMU) was built at Eastleigh in 1957 for operation on rural branch lines in Southern England. Originally numbered 1101 it later carried the number 205001 until withdrawn by Connex South Central in November 2004. It is pictured at Shepherdswell whilst still carrying Connex livery on 25 July 2005.

Author

CURRENT ELECTRIC LOCOMOTIVES & MULTIPLE UNITS

Name	Number	Builder	Type	Built	Comments
No.1		Kearsley Electric locomotive		1928	Ex- Electric Railway Museum, Coventry
	11161 / 11187	Southern Railway	Class 404 (COR)	1938	Unit number 3142 - two coaches remain of the original 4-car unit
	62385 (1399)	BREL	Class 421 (CIG)	1970-1972	Unit number 1399 - 1 coach remains of the original 4-car unit
	70904 / 76397 / 76398	British Rail	Class 423 (VOP)	1968	Unit number 3905 (Ex 4-VEP) - 3 coaches remain of the original 4-car unit
	76875	BREL	Class 423 (VEP)	1973-1974	Unit number 3545 - 1 coach remains of the original 4-car unit
	54000 / 67300	BREL	Class 210 / 316 / 457	1981 1989	Ex- Electric Railway Museum, Coventry. Part of unit 210001 / 316999 / 457001.

Locomotive No.1 was built in 1928 by Hawthorn Leslie for operation at Kearsley power station near Bolton. The locomotive was based at the Electric Railway Museum in Coventry, before moving to the East Kent Railway when the Electric Railway Museum closed. It is seen at Shepherdswell on 19 May 2019.

Author

Left: The 4-COR units were built for the Southern Railway in 1937/8 for main line electric services in Wessex and Sussex. They remained in service until 1972. The Southern Electric Group owns five carriages, including all four vehicles from unit 3142, two of which are located at the East Kent Railway, whilst the other three vehicles are located at a private restoration site at Sellindge in Kent. Being an electric unit, the 4-COR carriages operate with a diesel locomotive at the East Kent Railway. 4-COR 3142 vehicle 11187 is seen here at Shepherdswell on 14 July 2019.

Below: 4-COR 3142, meets 2-EPB 5759 and MLV 68001 at Shepherdswell on 7 September 2014.
Both: Phil Barnes

4-CIG (Class 421) (not pictured)

The Class 421 (CIG) units were built for mainline operations in the south-east of England between 1964 and 1972. Some units were provided with a buffet car and classified as 4-BIG (Class 422). They operated across Wessex, Sussex and Kent before being replaced by more modern rolling stock, the last unit being withdrawn in 2010. One carriage from four-car unit 1399 is preserved at the East Kent Railway and is usually marshalled with the three Class 423 4-VOP carriages, although they have not operated in traffic.

Above: The Class 423 units were built between 1967 and 1974 for outer suburban operations in the south-east of England. They operated on the Kent, Sussex and Wessex routes and were withdrawn in 2005, when they were replaced by new rolling stock.

The 4-VOP units were created by Connex South Central in 1998/99 for use on suburban services, which involved the removal of the seating compartments and the First-Class accommodation. Three vehicles from unit 3905 are restored at the East Kent Railway and are usually formed as a 4-car unit with the 4-CIG vehicle. The set is still being restored and has not yet operated in passenger service.

Vehicle 76875 from 4-VEP unit 3545 is preserved by the East Kent Railway. Being an electric unit, it usually operates with a diesel locomotive. It is seen at Shepherdswell on 19 May 2019.

Author

Right: The Class 457 vehicle now based at the East Kent Railway has a complicated history. It started life as part of an experimental Diesel Electric Multiple Unit (DEMU) built in 1981 by British Rail Engineering Limited (BREL) in Derby. The surviving vehicle was numbered 54000 and formed part of Unit 210001, which operated mainly on the Western Region.

In 1989 British Rail started to develop a new type of Electric Multiple Unit (EMU) which utilised some vehicles from the previous Class 210 unit. The carriage was renumbered 67300 and formed part of unit 316999, later 457001. The carriage was preserved at the Electric Railway Museum in Coventry, before moving to the East Kent Railway when the Electric Railway Museum closed in 2018. It is in the bay platform at Eythorne on 14 July 2019.

Phil Barnes

Carriages & Wagons

A former LMS Stanier carriage is used to house the Walmer Model Railway at Shepherdswell. Two former British Rail Mark 2 carriages, fitted with air brakes, are based on the railway and often operate on passenger service.

A General Utility Van (GUV), built by the Southern Railway in 1939 and rescued from Ramsgate railway depot in Kent, houses the tea room at Eythorne. There is also a selection of wagons located at the railway.

A unique Leyland experimental carriage was based at the East Kent Railway for a time. It was built in 1983 (RDB977091) by British Leyland and underwent trials on various routes around the UK. It left Shepherdswell for the Gwendraeth Valley Railway at Kidwelly in Carmarthenshire, where it remains.

Above: Mk 2f Open First 1215, in the platform at Shepherdswell on 10 May 2019.

Author

Left: An ex-Southern Railway brake van at Shepherdswell on 26 January 2020.

Peter Wilson Collection

FORMER STEAM LOCOMOTIVES

Name	Works Number	Builder	Type	Built	Comments
ALBERT	2248	Barclay	0-4-0ST	1948	Now at Plym Valley Railway
BROOKFIELD	2613	Bagnall	0-6-0PT	1940	Visiting locomotive. Now at Mangapps Farm Railway Museum
MINNIE	358	Fox/Walker	0-6-0ST	1878	Now at Mangapps Farm Railway Museum
SPITFIRE	1964	Barclay	0-4-0ST	1929	Now at Lincolnshire Wolds Railway

ST = Saddle Tank   PT = Pannier Tank

ALBERT was built by Andrew Barclay and Sons for the British Sugar Corporation in 1948 and worked at their plants in Worcester and Somerset. ALBERT moved to the Nene Valley Railway and then to the East Kent Railway. In 2004 the locomotive moved to the Plym Valley Railway. Here, it is seen at Shepherdswell in the early days of the railway.

Peter Wilson Collection

BROOKFIELD was built in 1940 by W G Barclay as a narrow-gauge locomotive (metre gauge) to work in Turkey but due to the onset of war the locomotive was diverted to the Admiralty Machinery Depot at Stoke-on-Trent, where it was used as a shunting engine. The depot closed in December 1959 but the locomotive was purchased by Brookfield Foundry, who took over the site, and remained there until 1982. BROOKFIELD was then preserved on the Pontypool and Blaenavon Railway in South Wales. Later the locomotive went on tour to the Gwili Railway, the Foxfield Railway and finally the East Kent Railway over the August 1996 Bank Holiday weekend, on which occasion it is pictured at Shepherdswell. BROOKFIELD can now be found at the Mangapps Farm Railway Museum in Essex.

Peter Wilson Collection

MINNIE (not pictured)

MINNIE was built by Fox / Walker in 1878 and worked at various industrial sites in North Yorkshire before being preserved. She spent around 20-years at the Kent and East Sussex Railway, before a brief visit to the East Kent Railway as a static exhibit. In 1993 MINNIE moved to the Mangapps Farm Railway Museum in Essex.

SPITFIRE was built in 1929 by Andrew Barclay and Sons and worked at various industrial sites around Manchester before being preserved. SPITFIRE spent several years at the East Kent Railway but is now in operation at the Lincolnshire Wolds Railway. The loco is seen at Shepherdswell preparing to work an Easter Bunny Special.

Peter Wilson Collection

FORMER DIESEL LOCOMOTIVES & DIESEL MULTIPLE UNITS

Name	Number	Builder	Type	Built	Comments
	09025 (D4113)	British Railways	0-6-0DE	1961	Now at the Lavender Line
	NS687	V/Foundry	0-6-0DE	1950	NS Class 600. Now in The Netherlands.
	01543	Thomas Hill	0-4-0DH	1982	Ex-Ministry of Defence, Kineton
R.J.MITCHELL	33063	Birmingham Railway & Wagon Company	Bo-Bo	1962	Now at the Spa Valley Railway
SEALION	33065	Birmingham Railway & Wagon Company	Bo-Bo	1962	Now at the Spa Valley Railway
	50256 / 56343 (101682)	Metro Cammell	Class 101	1957 1958	Now at the Wensleydale Railway
	52006 / 52031	British Railways	Class 107	1961	52006 now at Avon Valley Railway 52031 now at Tanat Valley Railway
	54224 / 51572	British Railways	Class 108	1960	54224 originally 56224. 54224 now at Keith & Dufftown Railway. 51572 now at Wensleydale Railway
	51562 / 51922	British Railways	Class 108	1960	National Railway Museum collection
	55033	Pressed Steel Company	Class 121	1960	Visited between September 1996 and April 1997. Now at Colne Valley Railway.
	437363	Ruston Hornsby	0-4-0DH	1960	
	08108	British Railways	0-6-0DE	1955	Now at Kent & East Sussex Railway
	226 (5261)	V/Foundry	0-4-0DM	1945	Now at Mangapps Farm Railway Museum
	D297 / 2583	V/Foundry / Drewry	0-4-0DM	1956	Now at Bressingham Steam Museum
	D2700	North British Locomotive Company	0-4-0DM	1955	Now at Whitwell and Reepham Railway
	2389	Hunslet	0-4-0DM	1941	Now at the Eden Valley Railway
DOUGAL	D77 / 2251	V/Foundry / Drewry	0-4-0DM	1947	Now at the Rother Valley Railway

DE = Diesel Electric   DM = Diesel Mechanical   DH – Diesel Hydraulic

Above: 09025 seen at Shepherdswell in Connex livery on 15 June 2014. For a period of time 09025 was painted in Connex livery on one side of the locomotive and green livery (with number D4113) on the other side.

Below: 09025 displays the green side of its livery as D4113 at Shepherdswell on 18 November 2012.

Both: Author

NS687 at Shepherdswell on 7 September 2014. This locomotive has now returned to The Netherlands.

Phil Barnes

Diesel Locomotives (not pictured)

08108

08108 was withdrawn by British Rail in 1984 and sold to a private operator in Newmarket, before moving to the East Kent Railway for a short period of time. The locomotive is now based at the Kent and East Sussex Railway.

Ruston-Hornsby 437363

Ruston-Hornsby locomotive number 437363, which was an ex-British Sugar locomotive, was located at the East Kent Railway for a period of time.

226 (5261)

226 was built by the Vulcan Foundry in 1945 and worked at various industrial locations before moving to the East Kent Railway in the early 1990s. The locomotive is now based at the Mangapps Farm Railway Museum in Essex.

D297 (2583)

D297 was built in 1951 at the Vulcan Foundry and was later stabled at Wymondham in Norfolk. The locomotive is understood to have been based at the East Kent Railway for a period of time before moving to the Bressingham Steam Museum.

2389

Locomotive number 2389 was built by Hunslet in 1941 and worked at various industrial sites. The locomotive is understood to have been based at the East Kent Railway for a while but is now located at the Eden Valley Railway.

D77 (2251) 'DOUGAL'

D77 was built by the Vulcan Foundry at Newton-Le-Willows in 1947 and worked at various industrial locations, before moving to the East Kent Railway. The locomotive moved to the Rother Valley Railway in September 2005.

Above: The two Class 33s, 33063 in blue nearest the camera and 33065 in grey primer behind, are stabled at Shepherdswell on 3 June 2002.

Phil Barnes

Below: 33065 SEALION arriving at Shepherdswell in May 2003.

Peter Wilson Collection

Above: 6583 (33063) at Eythorne in Summer 2003.

Below: 33063 at Shepherdswell in January 2003.

Both: Peter Wilson Collection

Above: D2700 was one of eight locomotives built by the North British Locomotive Company in 1955. The locomotive was based at the East Kent Railway for several years but has now moved to the Whitwell and Reepham Railway. Here it is shunting at Shepherdswell.

Below: D2700 shunting at Eythorne on the August Bank Holiday in 1996.

Both: Peter Wilson Collection

The Class 121 'Bubble Cars' were built by British Rail in 1960 for operating rural branch lines, originally on the Western Region. Car 55033 visited the East Kent Railway between September 1996 and April 1997. Both these pictures were taken at Shepherdswell.

Both: Peter Wilson Collection

A large fleet of Class 101 Diesel Multiple Units (DMUs) were built by Metro-Cammell between 1956 and 1959, and were very popular, operating for 47 years on the national network. Vehicles 50256 and 56343 (unit 101682) operated at the East Kent Railway between 2003 and 2016 before moving to the Wensleydale Railway. When the unit originally arrived at the East Kent Railway it was painted in Regional Railways Livery, but was later painted in all-over blue. The unit sometimes operated with a Class 108 vehicle to form a hybrid two-car unit or a three-car unit. The unit is seen in Regional Railways livery at Eythorne on the 24 July 2005 with a 'Wigmore Lane Halt' destination display.

Author

Above: The Class 101 unit arriving at Shepherdswell on 30 August 2015.

Below: Class 101 vehicle waits at Eythorne in the spring sunshine on 17 April 2016, on this occasion coupled to a Class 108 vehicle.

Both: Author

Class 107 DMU (not pictured)

A 2-car Class 107 DMU was based at the railway between 1992 and 1996. The Class 107 units were built by British Rail in Derby in 1960. Vehicles 52006 and 52031 operated in Scotland before moving to the East Kent Railway and carried an orange Strathclyde PTE livery.

A large fleet of Class 108 Diesel Multiple Units (DMUs) were built by British Rail in Derby between 1958 and 1961. They proved to be very popular and operated on the national network until 1993, with a number preserved at various heritage railways around the country. Two Class 108 units were based at the East Kent Railway at different times.

The first Class 108 unit arrived in July 1993 and stayed until December 1996. During this period, it was used to operate the first train on 24 June 1995. The unit was later remarshalled, with one carriage (54224 / 56224) now located at the Keith & Dufftown Railway and the other carriage (51572) now at the Wensleydale Railway.

A second Class 108 unit, formed of coaches 51562 / 51922 from the national collection, arrived in July 2014 but returned to the National Railway Museum in 2017 after repainting. The Class 108 vehicles were sometimes coupled with Class 101 vehicles to form a hybrid two-car unit or a three-car unit.

The Class 108 unit used for the opening train, is seen at Shepherdswell in the early days of the railway in Network SouthEast livery.

Peter Wilson Collection

Above: Class 108 vehicle at Eythorne on 17 April 2016, coupled to a Class 101 vehicle.

Author

Below: When the Class 108 unit from the National Railway Museum first arrived, one coach was painted blue and the other painted green. During its time at the East Kent Railway both carriages were painted blue. The unit is seen here at Shepherdswell in September 2014.

Phil Barnes

FORMER ELECTRIC MULTIPLE UNITS

Name	Number	Builder	Type	Built	Comments
	68001	British Railways	Class 419 (MLV)	1959	Now at Southall
	68002	British Railways	Class 419 (MLV)	1959	Now at Southall
	68008	British Railways	Class 419 (MLV)	1959	Now at Southall
	68009	British Railways	Class 419 (MLV)	1959	Now at Southall
	61229 / 61230 69013 / 70235	British Railways	Class 411/412 (CEP/BEP)	1958 1959	Unit 7105. 61229 / 61230 at Eastleigh. 69013 70235 at Epping & Ongar Railway
	10096 / 11825	Southern Railway	Class 404 (COR)	1937 1938	Now located at Sellindge in Kent
	65373 / 77558	British Rail	Class 416 (2-EPB)	1956	Unit 5759. Now at Southall

The Class 411 (CEP) units were originally built for main line operations in Kent between 1956 and 1963. Some units were provided with a buffet car and classified as Class 412 (BEP). They eventually operated across Wessex, Sussex and Kent before being replaced by more modern rolling stock, the last being withdrawn in 1995. The unit was located at the East Kent Railway for a number of years but has since moved elsewhere. The intention is to preserve a complete 4-BEP unit, two carriages of which are now at the Epping and Ongar Railway in Essex, whilst the other two vehicles are at Eastleigh being restored. 7105 4-BEP is pictured in South West trains livery at Shepherdswell in March 2010.

Peter Wilson Collection

The Class 416 2-EPB units were originally constructed between 1953 and 1956 for operation on British Railways' Southern Region and on Tyneside. The Tyneside units later moved to the South East to supplement the existing Class 415 (4-car) and 416 units. A number of units were fitted with window-bars and operated on the North London Line between Richmond and Broad Street / North Woolwich. The last units were retired in 1995, although passenger services finished a couple of years earlier. Unit 5759 was based on the East Kent Railway until 2016, when it moved to the Southall Railway Centre in London. It is seen, still with *Kent Link* branding at Shepherdswell on 7 August 1999.

Author

5759 seen arriving at Shepherdswell on 15 June 2014.

Author

Two views of 2-EPB 5759 in service as hauled stock during the EMU Gala on 7 September 2014. Above at Eythorne, below at Shepherdswell.

Both: Phil Barnes

Above: MLV 68001 stabled in the sidings at Shepherdswell on 15 June 2014.

Author

Below: MLV 68008 being shunted at Shepherdswell on 7 September 2014 .

Phil Barnes

Reconstruction

The railway was in a derelict state when the society took over the Shepherdswell site in 1989, but work started immediately on clearing the area and building new station platforms at Shepherdswell and Eythorne.

Permanent Way

The East Kent Railway is just over two miles long, with two stations, a tunnel and two level crossings to maintain. There is an enormous amount of work involved in maintaining the infrastructure and keeping lineside vegetation under control.

Rolling Stock

The railway now has a small enclosed shed at Shepherdswell, which has enabled some maintenance to take place indoors. A number of groups are based at the railway and take responsibility for the maintenance of specific items of rolling stock. These include the Southern Electric Group who look after the historic 4-COR vehicles.

Café and Shop Facilities

The 'Colonels Café' at Shepherdswell is very popular and opens Tuesday to Sunday all year round for the general public as well as railway visitors. There is also a station tea room at Eythorne, which also opens from Tuesday to Sunday and also sells a limited selection of toys and gifts. There is a more extensive gift shop located alongside the platform at Shepherdswell station.

Fares

As with many preserved railways, fares have to be competitive as there are many other attractions in the area. In 2003 the adult return fare was £5.00, which had increased to £7.00 by 2012, but was reduced to £6.00 in subsequent years. The adult return fare was £7.50 in 2019.

Timetables

The railway usually operates on Sundays from Easter to October and Saturdays in the school summer holidays. Brake van rides are also offered on Wednesdays during the school summer holidays. A number of special events are held throughout the year, often over Bank Holiday weekends and Santa Specials operate around the Christmas period.

The off-peak timetable usually consists of three return journeys from Shepherdswell, with four return trips on peak days. Special timetables operate when there are special events taking place. The journey time is fifteen minutes each way.

2019 Off Peak Timetable

Shepherdswell	11:30	13:10	14:30
Eythorne	11:45	13:25	14:45
Eythorne	12:05	13:45	15:10
Shepherdswell	12:20	14:00	15:25

2019 Peak Timetable

Shepherdswell	11:00	12:15	13:45	15:00
Eythorne	11:15	12:30	14:00	15:15
Eythorne	11:45	13:00	14:30	15:45
Shepherdswell	12:00	13:15	14:45	16:00

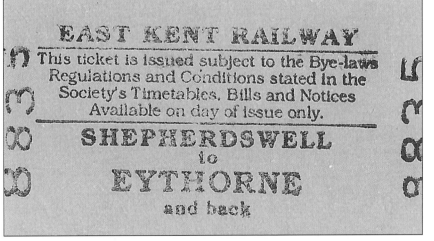

An 'Edmondson' style card ticket issued on 15 June 2014.
Author

Above: The new platform under construction at Eythorne.

Dave Harris / EKR

Below: RICHBOROUGH CASTLE working a maintenance train on 9 May 2013.

Peter Wilson Collection

Above: After several years hard work the railway finally reopened on 24 June 1995. A Class 108 unit operated the first train and is seen breaking through a 'First Train' banner.

Below: The first train shortly after arrival at Eythorne on 24 June 1995.

Both: Dave Harris / EKR

SPECIAL EVENTS

A number of special events are held at the railway over the year. These have evolved over the years and now include a Craft Weekend, Beer Festival and Santa Specials. Fish and Chip Supper Trains run on certain days, as well as afternoon Cream Tea trains.

SPITFIRE, an 0-4-0 Barclay locomotive built in 1929, preparing to work an Easter Bunny Special at Shepherdswell. The Easter Bunny Specials have now been replaced by 'Travel for £2 days', which have proved to be very popular.

Peter Wilson Collection

Above: A Southend Transport Leyland Tiger PD3 at Eythorne during a Classic Vehicles Event in conjunction with the nearby Dover Transport Museum. The vintage bus service connected Eythorne station with the Dover Transport Museum.

Author

Below: 2-EPB 5759 (in use as hauled stock) and 4-COR 3142 at Shepherdswell during the Electric Multiple Unit Gala on 7 September 2014.

Phil Barnes

Above: Andrew Barclay 0-4-0 SPITFIRE seen at Shepherdswell on 7 August 1999 during a 'Thomas the Tank Engine' event.

Left: AD427 THE BUFFS seen at Shepherdswell on the same occasion.

Both: Author

Above: A special event was held on 7th October 2016 to advertise the Knees Woodland with former MOD locomotive 01543.

Matthew Plews / EKR

Below: AD427 THE BUFFS waits to leave Eythorne with the 1110 to Shepherdswell during a Teddy Bears' Picnic event on 3 June 2002. Barclay 0-4-0ST ALBERT is at the rear of the train.

Phil Barnes

MINIATURE RAILWAYS

There are two miniature railways at Shepherdswell, both of which usually operate on railway operating days.

Elevated Miniature Railway (3½ and 5-inch gauge)

A 3½ and five-inch gauge elevated miniature railway was constructed in the early days of the railway. There is a small station located near to the site entrance, above the main station and a small shed at the far end of the line. A number of different locomotives have operated the railway over the years.

Left: 0-4-0 North British locomotive built by Maxitrak leaving the station on 24 July 2005.

Author

Below: A Class 33 'Crompton' locomotive, built by Bexhill Model Engineering Supplies, seen in May 2003.

Peter Wilson Collection

LMS Ivatt 2-6-2T Number 41209 on 12 March 2010.
Peter Wilson Collection

D5908 (Class 23) 'Baby Deltic' at the station on 30 August 2015.
Author

A tram and carriage on the 5-inch gauge line on 30 August 2015.
Author

The Knees Woodland Miniature Railway
(7¼ inch gauge)

The Knees Woodland Miniature Railway was officially opened on 24 August 2014 and has gradually been extended since, with a new extension opening in 2019. A section of the former footbridge from Gravesend station in Kent has been used to create a bridge over a small pond. A number of locomotives are based on the railway, which usually opens when the main line service is running.

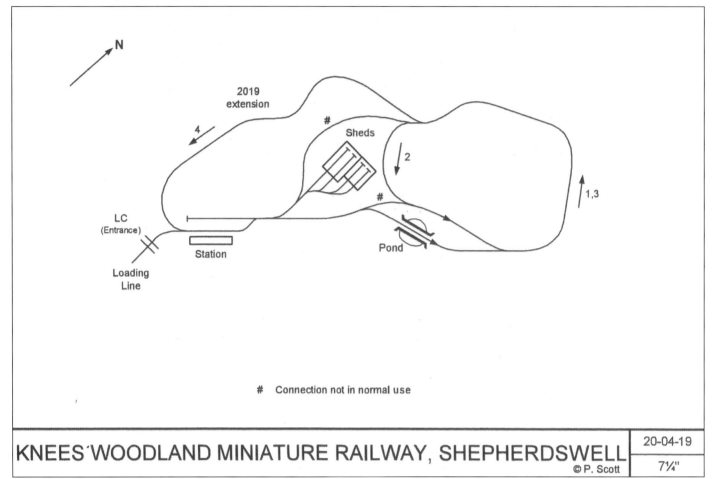

\#   Connection not in normal use

KNEES WOODLAND MINIATURE RAILWAY, SHEPHERDSWELL

20-04-19

© P. Scott   7¼"

Copyright Peter Scott

CURRENT ROLLING STOCK LIST

Name	Number	Type	Comments
PLANET		0-4-0	Petrol Hydrostatic
	7	0-4-0	Petrol locomotive
GOLIATH		0-4-0	Battery Locomotive
	4	0-4-0	Petrol Hydrostatic
POPPY		0-4-0	Battery Locomotive
		Bo-Bo	Battery Locomotive (Metropolitan Electric Locomotive)
	8	0-4-0	Hudson diesel hydrostatic
		0-4-0	Lister Diesel

Above: PLANET, a 0-4-0 petrol hydrostatic locomotive, arriving at the main station on opening day, 24 August 2014.

Right: D7083 ANTHONY KEENE TONY visited the Knees Woodland Railway for the opening day on 24 August 2014. At this point the balloon loop had not been completed, so a temporary platform and siding were laid in the woods.

Both: Author

Above: The station area seen on 17 April 2016, with the 0-4-0 Lister diesel waiting in the siding.

Below: The two 0-4-0 petrol hydrostatic locomotives at the station on 19 May 2019.

Both: Author

Above: The sheds at the Knees Woodland Railway seen on 19 May 2019. The railway was originally intended to have a mixed 5 and 7¼ inch gauge track, hence some mixed gauge line near the sheds.

Right: The 0-4-0 Lister diesel waiting outside the sheds on 19 May 2019.

Both: Author

Above: On the approach to Shepherdswell station there is a display of mining trucks, several recovered from local coal mines, seen on 30 August 2015.

Author

Below: In March 2014 the foundations of what is believed to be the original Colonel Stephens well and workshop were discovered near the Knees Woodland, seen here in July 2019.

Phil Barnes

Above: A mine tub from Betteshanger Colliery, used for moving waste from the boiler house, seen on 18 November 2012.

Author

Below: Coal mining display outside Eythorne station on 11 January 2020.

Peter Wilson

Above: When Gravesend station in Kent was remodelled over Christmas 2013, three sections of the former station footbridge were delivered to the East Kent Railway. One section has been used as a bridge by the Knees Woodland Railway, one is being used as a viewing platform alongside the Colonel Stephens well and workshop excavation, whilst the final section will be used as a viewing platform alongside Shepherdswell station. Here we see two sections of the footbridge at Shepherdswell on 15 June 2014.

Below: By 19 May 2019, this section of the footbridge was in use as a viewing platform at Shepherdswell.

Both: Author

Former Bradford Trolleybus number 704, called "Barney", is in the process of being restored at Shepherdswell. These two views show the good progress made in the five years between the two pictures (15 June 2014 and 19 May 2019).

Both: Author

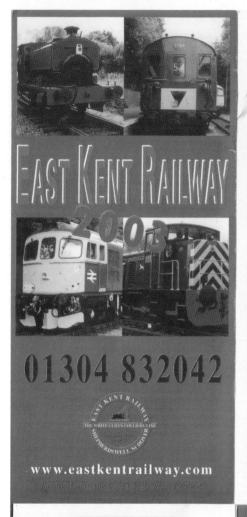

East Kent Railway

01304 832042

www.eastkentrailway.com

East Kent Railway

Timetable and Information 2012

www.eastkentrailway.co.uk

EAST KENT RAILWAY TRUST
Registered Charity No. 1095790

East Kent Railway

EKR

The Kent Colliery Line

Shepherdswell, Dover. Registered Charity No. 1095790

A fun and affordable day out for all the family!

2014

Tel: 01304 832042

enquiries@eastkentrailway.co.uk

www.eastkentrailway.co.uk

Registered charity No. 1095790

East Kent Railway

EKR

The Kent Colliery Line

A fun and affordable day out for all the family!

2016

Tel: 01304 832042

enquiries@eastkentrailway.co.uk

www.eastkentrailway.co.uk

Registered charity No. 1095790

The Knees Woodlands

At

East Kent Railway

www.eastkentrailway.co.uk

EAST KENT RAILWAY TRUST

Registered Charity No. 1095790

East Kent Railway

EKR

The Kent Colliery Line

A fun and affordable day out for all the family!

2019

Celebrating 30 years

Tel: 01304 832042

enquiries@eastkentrailway.co.uk

www.eastkentrailway.co.uk

Registered charity No. 1095790